HOLY ROSARY

St Josemaría Escrivá

HOLY ROSARY

Scepter

London – New York

This edition of *Holy Rosary* is published:
in England by Scepter (U.K.) Ltd, 21 Hinton Avenue,
    Hounslow, TW4 6AP; e-mail: scepter@pobox.com
in the U.S. by Scepter Publishers Inc.; 800-322-8773; e-mail:
    info@scepterpublishers.org; www.scepterpublishers.org

This is a translation of *Santo Rosario*, first published in Spain in
1934.
© Original – Fundación Studium, Madrid
© Translation – Fundación Studium, Madrid, 2003
© This edition – Scepter, London, 2019
The illustrations are by L. Borobio.

With ecclesiastical approval

Scepter (U.K.): ISBN 978 0 906138 65 6
Scepter Publishers Inc.: ISBN 978 1 88933492 9

Cover design & typeset by KIP Intermedia, and printed in England.

THE AUTHOR

Saint Josemaría Escrivá de Balaguer was born in Barbastro, in northern Spain, on 9 January 1902. He started his ecclesiastical studies in the Seminary of Logroño in 1918, and later, in 1920, in that of Saint Francis de Paula in Saragossa. Between 1923 and 1927 he studied Civil Law in the University of Saragossa. He was ordained to the priesthood on 28 March 1925. He began his work as a priest in the village of Perdiguera, within the diocese of Saragossa, and afterwards in Saragossa itself.

In the spring of 1927, he moved to the Spanish capital, Madrid, and there carried out abundant priestly work, devoting attention also to the poor and destitute in the outlying districts of the city, and especially to the incurably sick and the dying in the hospitals. He worked as chaplain for the *Patronato de Enfermos* (Foundation for the Sick), a welfare organization run by the Apostolic Sisters of the Sacred Heart. He also taught at a university academy, and continued his studies for a doctorate in Civil Law.

On 2 October 1928, God let him see Opus Dei (in English, the Work of God). By divine inspiration, on 14 February 1930 he understood that the apostolic work of Opus Dei also needed to include women. As a result, a new path was opening up in the Church to foster, among people from all social classes, the effort to attain holiness and to carry out apostolate, through the sanctification of ordinary work, in the midst of the world. On 14 February 1943, he founded the Priestly Society of the Holy Cross, which is inseparably united to Opus Dei and which, as well as opening up the possibility of ordaining lay members of Opus Dei to the priesthood and incardinating them for the service of the Work, would later on also enable priests who are incardinated in dioceses to share in Opus Dei's spirituality and asceticism, seeking holiness in the exercise of their ministerial duties, while remaining exclusively under their respective Ordinaries. Opus Dei was established as a Personal Prelature by Saint John Paul II on 28 November 1982. This was the canonical formula foreseen and desired by Saint Josemaría Escrivá.

In 1946 he took up residence in Rome, which was to be his home for the rest of his life. From there, he encouraged and guided the development of Opus Dei throughout the world, using all his energies to give to the men and women of Opus Dei a solid formation in doctrine, ascetical spirit and apostolate. At the time of his death, Opus Dei had more than 60,000 members from 80 different nationalities.

Saint Josemaría died on 26 June 1975. For years, he had been offering his life for the Church and for the Pope. His mortal remains rest beneath the altar of the prelatic church of Our Lady of Peace, in the central offices of the Prelature of Opus Dei. The reputation for holiness which the Founder of Opus Dei enjoyed in his lifetime has spread after his death to the far corners of the earth, as can be seen from countless spiritual and material favours attributed to his intercession; among them, a number of cures which are medically inexplicable. Saint John Paul II canonized Josemaría Escrivá on 6 October 2002.

His published writings, apart from the theological and legal study *La Abadesa de la Huelgas*, include books of spirituality which have been translated into many different languages: *The Way, Holy Rosary, Christ is Passing By, Friends of God, The Way of the Cross, In Love with the Church, Furrow, The Forge* and *In Dialogue with the Lord* (the last six titles have been published posthumously).. Another book published under his name is *Conversations with Monsignor Escrivá*, which brings together interviews he gave to members of the press. A wide range of documentation on Saint Josemaría can be found at www.escrivaworks.org and at www.opusdei.org.

Today, as in other times,
the Rosary must be
a powerful weapon
to enable us to win in our interior struggle,
and to help all souls.
Exalt holy Mary with your tongue:
God asks you for reparation,
and for praise from your lips.
May you always want and know how to spread
peace and happiness throughout the world,
through this beautiful devotion to our Lady
and through your watchful love.

ST JOSEMARÍA ESCRIVÁ
Rome, October 1968

To say the Holy Rosary,
considering the mysteries,
repeating the Our Father and Hail Mary,
with the praises to the Blessed Trinity
and the constant invocation of the Mother of God,
is a continuous act of faith, hope and love,
of adoration and reparation.

ST JOSEMARÍA ESCRIVÁ
Rome, 9 January 1973

These lines are not written for "little women." –They are written for full-grown men, and very... manly men, who at times, no doubt, have raised their hearts to God, crying out to Him with the Psalmist: *Notam fac mihi viam, in qua ambulem; quia ad te levavi animam meam.* –Teach me the way I should go, for to you I lift up my soul (Ps 143:8).

I must tell these men a secret that may very well be the beginning of the way that Christ wants them to follow.

My friend, if you want to be great, become little.

To be little it is necessary to believe as children believe, to love as children love, to give yourself up as children give themselves up... to pray as children pray.

And you have to do all this if you are to achieve what I am going to reveal to you in these lines:

The beginning of the way, at the end of which you will find yourself completely carried away by love for Jesus, is a trusting love for Mary.

–Do you want to love our Lady? –Well, then, get to know her. How? –By praying her Rosary *well.*

But, in the Rosary... we always say the same things! –Always the same? And don't people in love always say the same things to each other?... Might it not be that you find the Rosary monotonous because, instead of pronouncing words like a man, you mumble noises while your mind is very far from God?

–Moreover, listen: before each decade we are told the mystery to be *contemplated*.

–Have you... ever *contemplated* these mysteries?

Become little. Come with me and – this is the essence of what I want to tell you – we shall live the life of Jesus, Mary and Joseph.

Each day we shall do something new for them. We shall hear their family conversation. We shall see the Messiah grow up. We shall admire his thirty years of hidden life... We shall be present at his Passion and Death... We will be amazed at the glory of his Resurrection... In a word: carried away by Love (the only real love is Love), we shall contemplate each and every moment of the life of Christ.

For you, my friend, the reader of this book: I have written the *Holy Rosary* to help you and me become absorbed in prayer when we pray to our Lady.

Don't let the sound of words disturb you as you meditate on these thoughts: don't read them aloud, for then they would lose their intimacy.

But do pronounce the Our Father and the Hail Marys of each decade clearly and without rushing: this will help you always to get more and more out of this way of loving Mary.

And don't forget to pray for me.

THE AUTHOR
Rome, on the Feast of the Purification,
2 February 1952

My experience as a priest tells me that each soul has his own path to follow. Nonetheless, dear reader, I am going to give you some practical advice which will not stifle the work of the Holy Spirit within you, if you follow it prudently.

Pause for a few seconds – three or four – in silent meditation to consider each mystery of the Rosary before you recite the Our Father and the Hail Marys of that decade. I am sure this practice will increase your recollection and the fruits of your prayer.

And don't forget to pray for me.

THE AUTHOR
Rome, on the Feast of the Nativity of Our Lady,
8 September 1971

THE FIRST JOYFUL MYSTERY

THE ANNUNCIATION

Don't forget, my friend, that we are children. The Lady of the sweet name, Mary, is withdrawn in prayer.

You, in that house, are whatever you wish to be: a friend, a servant, an onlooker, a neighbour... –For the moment I don't dare to be anything. I hide behind you and, full of awe, I watch what is happening:

The Archangel delivers his message... *Quomodo fiet istud, quoniam virum non cognosco?* –But how can this come about since I am a virgin? (Luke 1:34)

Our Mother's voice reminds me – by contrast – of all the impurities of men.... mine too.

And then how I hate those low, mean things of the earth...What resolutions!

Fiat mihi secundum verbum tuum. –Let it be done to me according to your word (Luke 1:38). At the enchantment of this virginal phrase, the Word became flesh.

The first decade is about to end... I still have time to tell my God, before anyone else does: 'Jesus, I love You.'

THE SECOND JOYFUL MYSTERY

THE VISITATION

By now, my little friend, you have no doubt learned to manage on your own. –Joyfully keep Joseph and Mary company... and you will hear the traditions of the House of David:

You will hear about Elizabeth and Zachary, you will be moved by Joseph's pure love, and your heart will pound whenever they mention the Child who will be born in Bethlehem...

We walk in haste towards the mountains, to a town of the tribe of Judah (Luke 1:39).

We arrive. –It is the house where John the Baptist is to be born. –Elizabeth gratefully hails the Mother of her Redeemer: Blessed art thou amongst women and blessed is the fruit of thy womb! –Why should I be honoured with a visit from the mother of my Lord? (Luke 1:42-43)

The unborn Baptist quivers... (Luke 1:41) –Mary's humility pours forth in the *Magnificat*... –And you and I, who are proud – who were proud – promise to be humble.

THE THIRD JOYFUL MYSTERY

THE BIRTH OF OUR LORD

Caesar Augustus has issued a decree for a census to be taken of the whole world. For this purpose, every person must go to the city of his ancestors. –And since Joseph belongs to the house and line of David, he goes with the Virgin Mary from Nazareth to the town of David called Bethlehem, in Judea (Luke 2:1-5).

And in Bethlehem is born our God: Jesus Christ! –There is no room at the inn: He is born in a stable. –And his Mother wraps him in swaddling clothes and lays him in a manger (Luke 2:7).

Cold. –Poverty... –I am Joseph's little servant. –How good Joseph is! –He treats me like a son. –He even forgives me if I take the Child in my arms and spend hour after hour saying sweet and loving things to him!...

And I kiss him – you kiss him too! – and I rock him in my arms, and I sing to him and call him King, Love, my God, my Only-One, my All!... How beautiful is the Child... and how short the decade!

THE FOURTH JOYFUL MYSTERY

THE PRESENTATION

When the time has come for the Mother's purification, in accordance with the Law of Moses, the Child must be taken to Jerusalem to be presented to the Lord (Luke 2:22).

And this time it will be you, my friend, who carries the cage with the doves. –Just think: she – Mary Immaculate! – submits to the Law as if she were defiled.

Through this example, foolish child, won't you learn to fulfil the holy Law of God, regardless of any personal sacrifice?

Purification! You and I certainly do need purification! –Atonement, and more than atonement, Love. –Love as a searing iron to cauterize our souls' uncleanness, and as a fire to kindle with divine flames the wretchedness of our hearts.

An upright and devout man has come to the Temple led by the Holy Spirit (it had been revealed to him that he would not die until he had set eyes on the Christ). –He takes the Messiah into his arms and says to him: Now, my Lord, you can let your servant go from this world in peace, just as you promised... because my eyes have seen the Saviour (Luke 2:25-30).

THE FIFTH JOYFUL MYSTERY

THE FINDING IN THE TEMPLE

Where is Jesus? —The Child, my Lady!... where is He?

Mary is crying. —In vain you and I have run from group to group, from caravan to caravan: no one has seen him. —Joseph, after useless attempts to keep from crying, cries too... And you... And I.

Being a common little fellow, I cry my eyes out and wail to heaven and earth... to make up for those times when I lost him through my own fault and did not cry.

Jesus: may I never lose you again... Now you and I are united in misfortune and grief, as we were united in sin. And from the depths of our being come sighs of heartfelt sorrow and burning phrases which the pen cannot and should not record.

And, once we are consoled by the joy of finding Jesus – three days he was gone! – debating with the teachers of Israel (Luke 2:46), you and I shall be left deeply impressed by the duty to leave our home and family to serve our heavenly Father.

THE FIRST SORROWFUL MYSTERY

THE AGONY IN THE GARDEN

Pray, that you may not enter into temptation. –And Peter fell asleep. –And the other apostles. –And you, little friend, fell asleep..., and I too was another sleepy-headed Peter.

Jesus, alone and sad, suffers and soaks the earth with his blood.

Kneeling on the hard ground, he perseveres in prayer... He weeps for you... and for me. The weight of the sins of men overwhelms him.

Pater, si vis, transfer calicem istum a me. –Father, if you are willing, remove this cup from me... Yet not my will, *sed tua fiat*, but yours be done (Luke 22:42).

An Angel from heaven comforts him. –Jesus is in agony. –He continues *prolixius*, praying more intensely... –He comes over to us and finds us asleep: Rise, he says again, and pray that you may not enter into temptation (Luke 22:46).

Judas the traitor: a kiss. –Peter's sword gleams in the night. –Jesus speaks: Have you come out as against a robber, with swords and clubs to capture me? (Mark 14:48)

We are cowards: we follow him from afar, but awake and praying. –Prayer... Prayer...

THE SECOND SORROWFUL MYSTERY

THE SCOURGING AT THE PILLAR

Pilate speaks: It is your custom that I release one prisoner to you at the Passover. Whom shall I set free, Barabbas – a thief jailed with others for a murder – or Jesus? (Matt 27:17) The crowd spurred on by their rulers cry: Put this man to death and release Barabbas (Luke 23:18).

Pilate speaks again: What shall I do, then, with Jesus who is called Christ? (Matt 27:22) *–Crucifige eum!* Crucify him! (Mark 15:14)

Pilate, for the third time, says to them: Why, what evil has he done? I have found no crime in him deserving death (Luke 23:22).

The clamour of the mob grows louder: Crucify him, crucify him! (Mark 15:14)

And Pilate, wanting to please the crowd, releases Barabbas to them and orders Jesus to be scourged.

Bound to the pillar. Covered with wounds.

The blows of the lash sound upon his torn flesh, upon his undefiled flesh, which suffers for your sinful flesh. –More blows. More fury. Still more... It is the last extreme of human cruelty.

Finally, exhausted, they untie Jesus. –And the body of Christ yields to pain and falls limp, broken and half dead.

You and I cannot speak. –Words are not needed. –Look at him, look at him... slowly. After this... can you ever fear penance?

THE THIRD SORROWFUL MYSTERY

REX JUDEOR

THE CROWNING WITH THORNS

Our King's eagerness for suffering has been fully satisfied!

—They lead my Lord to the courtyard of the palace, and there call together the whole troop (Mark 15:16). —The brutal soldiers strip his most pure body. —They drape a dirty purple rag about Jesus. —A reed, as a sceptre, in his right hand...

The crown of thorns, driven in by blows, makes him a mock king... *Ave Rex Judeorum!* —Hail, King of the Jews (Mark 15:18). And with their blows they wound his head. And they strike him... and spit on him.

Crowned with thorns and clothed in rags of purple, Jesus is shown to the Jewish crowd: *Ecce Homo!* —Here is the Man! And again the chief priests and their attendants raise the cry, saying: Crucify him, crucify him (John 19:5-6).

—You and I..., haven't we crowned him anew with thorns, and struck him and spat on him?

Never again, Jesus, never again... And a firm and practical resolution marks the end of these ten Hail Marys.

THE FOURTH SORROWFUL MYSTERY

THE CARRYING OF THE CROSS

C arrying His Cross, Jesus goes towards Calvary – called Golgotha in Hebrew (John 19:17). –And they lay hold of a certain Simon of Cyrene, who is coming in from the country; and they make him take the Cross and carry it behind Jesus (Luke 23:26).

The prophecy of Isaiah (53:12) has been fulfilled: *cum sceleratis reputatus est*, he was counted among the wicked: for two others, who were robbers, were led out with him to be put to death (Luke 23:32).

If anyone would follow me... Little friend: we are sad, living the Passion of our Lord Jesus. –See how lovingly he embraces the Cross. –Learn from him. –Jesus carries the Cross for you: you... carry it for Jesus.

But don't drag the Cross... Carry it squarely on your shoulder, because your Cross, if you carry it like that, will not be just any Cross: it will be... the Holy Cross. Don't carry your Cross with resignation: resignation is not a generous word. Love the Cross. When you really love it, your Cross will be... a Cross, without a Cross.

And surely you will find Mary on the way, just as Jesus did.

THE FIFTH SORROWFUL MYSTERY

THE CRUCIFIXION

For Jesus of Nazareth, King of the Jews, the throne of triumph is ready. You and I do not see him writhe on being nailed: suffering all that can be suffered, he spreads his arms in the gesture of an eternal Priest...

The soldiers take his holy garments and divide them into four parts. —In order not to tear the tunic, they cast lots to decide whose it shall be. —And so, once more, the words of Scripture are fulfilled: They have parted my garments among them, and for my clothes they cast lots (John 19:23-24).

Now he is on high... And close to her Son, at the foot of the Cross, stand Mary... and Mary, the wife of Cleophas, and Mary Magdalen. And John, the disciple Jesus loved. *Ecce mater tua!* —Behold your mother!: He gives us his Mother to be our Mother.

Earlier they had offered him wine mingled with gall, and when he had tasted it, he would not drink it (Matt 27:34).

Now he thirsts... for love, for souls.

Consummatum est. –It is accomplished (John 19:30).

Foolish child, look: all this... he has suffered it all for you... and for me. –Can you keep from crying?

THE FIRST GLORIOUS MYSTERY

THE RESURRECTION OF OUR LORD

When the Sabbath was over, Mary Magdalen and Mary, the mother of James, and Salome bought spices with which to go and anoint the dead body of Jesus. –Very early on the following day, just as the sun is rising, they come to the tomb (Mark 16:1-2). And on entering it they are dismayed, for they cannot find the body of our Lord. –A youth, clothed in white, says to them: Do not be afraid. I know you seek Jesus of Nazareth: *non est hic, surrexit enim sicut dixit*, he is not here, for he has risen, as he said (Matt 28:5).

He has risen! –Jesus has risen. He is not in the tomb. –Life has overcome death.

He appeared to his most holy Mother. –He appeared to Mary of Magdala, who is carried away by love. –And to Peter and the rest of the Apostles. –And to you and me, who are his disciples and more in love than Mary Magdalen: the things we say to him!

May we never die through sin; may our spiritual resurrection be eternal. –And before this decade is over, you have kissed the wounds in his feet..., and I, more daring – because I am more a child – have placed my lips upon his open side.

THE SECOND GLORIOUS MYSTERY

THE ASCENSION OF OUR LORD

Now the Master is teaching his disciples: he has opened their minds to understand the Scriptures, and he appoints them witnesses of his life and his miracles, of his Passion and Death, and of the glory of his Resurrection (Luke 24:45 and 48).

Then, he brings them out as far as the outskirts of Bethany, and blesses them. –And, as he does so, he withdraws from them and is carried up to heaven (Luke 24:51) until a cloud takes him out of their sight (Acts 1:9).

Jesus has gone to the Father. –Two Angels in white approach us and say: Men of Galilee, why do you stand looking up to heaven? (Acts 1:11)

Peter and the others go back to Jerusalem – *cum gaudio magno* – with great joy (Luke 24:52). –It is fitting that the Sacred Humanity of Christ should receive the homage, the praise and adoration of all the hierarchies of the Angels and of all the legions of the Blessed in Heaven.

But, you and I feel like orphans: we are sad, and we go to Mary for consolation.

THE THIRD GLORIOUS MYSTERY

THE DESCENT OF THE HOLY SPIRIT

Our Lord had said: I shall ask the Father, and he will give you another Advocate, another Consoler, to be with you forever (John 14:16). The disciples were gathered together in one room when suddenly they heard what sounded like a powerful wind from heaven, the noise of which filled the entire house where they were assembled. –At the same time something appeared that seemed like tongues of fire; these separated and came to rest on the head of each of them (Acts 2:1-3).

The Apostles were so filled with the Holy Spirit, that they seemed to be drunk (Acts 2:13).

Then Peter stood up with the eleven and addressed the people in a loud voice. –We, people from a hundred nations, hear him. –Each of us hears him in his own language. –You and I in ours. –He speaks to us of Christ Jesus and of the Holy Spirit and of the Father.

He is not stoned nor thrown in prison: of those who have heard him, three thousand are converted and baptized.

You and I, after helping the Apostles administer baptism, bless God the Father, for his Son Jesus, and we too feel drunk with the Holy Spirit.

THE FOURTH GLORIOUS MYSTERY

THE ASSUMPTION

Assumpta est Maria in coelum: gaudent angeli! –God has taken Mary – body and soul – to heaven: and the Angels rejoice!

So sings the Church. –And so, with that same cry of joy, we begin our contemplation in this decade of the Holy Rosary:

The Mother of God has fallen asleep. –Around her bed are the twelve Apostles. –Matthias in the place of Judas.

And we, through a grace respected by all, are also at her side.

But Jesus wants to have his Mother, body and soul, in heaven. –And the heavenly court, arrayed in all its splendour, greets our Lady. –You and I – children after all – take the train of Mary's magnificent blue cloak, and so we can watch the marvellous scene.

The most Blessed Trinity receives and showers honours on the Daughter, Mother, and Spouse of God... –And so great is our Lady's majesty that the Angels exclaim: Who is she?

THE FIFTH GLORIOUS MYSTERY

THE CROWNING OF THE BLESSED VIRGIN

You are all fair and without blemish. –You are a garden enclosed, my sister, my Bride, an enclosed garden, a sealed fountain. *–Veni: coronaberis*. –Come: you shall be crowned (Song of Songs 4:7, 12 and 8).

If you and I had been able, we too would have made her Queen and Lady of all creation.

A great sign appeared in heaven: a woman with a crown of twelve stars upon her head. –Adorned with the sun. –The moon at her feet (Rev 12:1). Mary, Virgin without stain, has made up for the fall of Eve: and she has crushed the head of hell's serpent with her immaculate heel. Daughter of God, Mother of God, Spouse of God.

The Father, the Son, and the Holy Spirit crown her as the rightful Empress of the Universe.

And the Angels pay her homage as her subjects... and the patriarchs and prophets and Apostles... and the martyrs and confessors and virgins and all the saints... and all sinners and you and I.

THE LITANY

Now the chorus of praise bursts forth in all its splendour of new light and variety of colour and meaning.

We call upon the Lord, upon Christ; we petition each of the divine Persons, and the most Holy Trinity; we speak words of ardent love to Mary: Mother of Christ, Mother most pure, Mother of good counsel, Mother of our Creator, Mother of our Saviour... Virgin most prudent... Seat of Wisdom, Mystical Rose, Tower of David, Ark of the Covenant, Morning Star... Refuge of sinners, Comforter of the afflicted, Help of Christians...

And the recognition of her reign – *Regina!*: Queen! – and of her mediation: *Sub tuum praesidium confugimus:* we fly to your protection, O holy Mother of God..., deliver us from all dangers, O ever glorious and blessed Virgin.

Pray for us, Queen of the most Holy Rosary, that we may be made worthy of the promises of our Lord Jesus Christ.

THE LITANY

Kyrie, eleison.
Kyrie eleison.
Christe, eleison.
Christe, eleison.
Kyrie, eleison.
Kyrie, eleison.
Christe, audi nos.
Christe, audi nos.
Christe, exaudi nos.
Christe, exaudi nos.

Lord, have mercy,
Lord, have mercy.
Christ, have mercy,
Christ, have mercy.
Lord, have mercy,
Lord, have mercy.
Christ hear us,
Christ graciously hear us.

Pater de caelis, Deus,
miserere nobis.
Fili, redemptor mundi Deus,

Spiritus Sancte, Deus,
Sancta Trinitas, unus Deus,
Sancta Maria, *ora pro nobis.*
Sancta Dei Genetrix,
Sancta Virgo virginum,
Mater Christi,
Mater Ecclesiae,
Mater divinae gratiae,
Mater purissima,

God the Father of heaven,
have mercy on us.
God the Son, Redeemer of
the world,
God the Holy Spirit,
Holy Trinity, one God,
Holy Mary, *pray for us.*
Holy Mother of God,
Holy Virgin of virgins,
Mother of Christ,
Mother of the Church,
Mother of divine grace,
Mother most pure,

Mater castissima,	Mother most chaste,
Mater inviolata,	Mother inviolate,
Mater intemerata,	Mother undefiled,
Mater amabilis,	Mother most lovable,
Mater admirabilis,	Mother most admirable,
Mater boni consilii,	Mother of good counsel,
Mater Creatoris,	Mother of our Creator,
Mater Salvatoris,	Mother of our Saviour,
Virgo prudentissima,	Virgin most prudent,
Virgo veneranda,	Virgin most venerable,
Virgo praedicanda,	Virgin most renowned,
Virgo potens,	Virgin most powerful,
Virgo clemens,	Virgin most merciful,
Virgo fidelis,	Virgin most faithful,
Speculum iustitiae,	Mirror of justice,
Sedes sapientiae,	Seat of wisdom,
Causa nostrae laetitiae,	Cause of our joy,
Vas spirituale,	Spiritual vessel,
Vas honorabile,	Vessel of honour,
Vas insigne devotionis,	Singular vessel of devotion,
Rosa mystica,	Mystical rose,
Turris Davidica,	Tower of David,
Turris eburnea,	Tower of ivory,
Domus aurea,	House of gold,
Foederis arca,	Ark of the covenant,
Ianua caeli,	Gate of heaven,
Stella matutina,	Morning star,
Salus infirmorum,	Health of the sick,
Refugium peccatorum,	Refuge of sinners,
Consolatrix afflictorum,	Comforter of the afflicted,
Auxilium christianorum,	Help of Christians,
Regina angelorum,	Queen of Angels,

Regina patriarcharum,	Queen of Patriarchs,
Regina prophetarum,	Queen of Prophets,
Regina apostolorum,	Queen of Apostles,
Regina martyrum,	Queen of Martyrs,
Regina confessorum,	Queen of Confessors,
Regina virginum,	Queen of Virgins,
Regina sanctorum omnium,	Queen of all Saints,
Regina sine labe originali concepta,	Queen conceived without original sin,
Regina in caelum assumpta,	Queen assumed into heaven,
Regina sacratissimi rosarii,	Queen of the most holy rosary,
Regina familiae,	Queen of the family,
Regina pacis,	Queen of peace,
Agnus Dei, qui tollis peccata mundi,	Lamb of God, you take away the sins of the world,
parce nobis, Domine.	*Spare us, O Lord.*
Agnus Dei, qui tollis peccata mundi,	Lamb of God, you take away the sins of the world,
exaudi nos, Domine.	*Graciously hear us, O Lord.*
Agnus Dei, qui tollis peccata mundi,	Lamb of God, you take away the sins of the world,
miserere nobis.	*Have mercy on us.*

My friend: I have told you just part of my secret. It is up to you, with God's help, to discover the rest. Take courage. Be faithful.

Become little. Our Lord hides himself from the proud and reveals the treasures of his grace to the humble.

Don't worry if, when thinking on your own, daring and childish words and affections arise in your heart. This is what Jesus wants and Mary is encouraging. If you say the Rosary in this way, you will learn to pray well.

APPENDIX

THE MYSTERIES OF LIGHT

Introductory Note

In his Apostolic Letter *Rosarium Virginis Mariae*, the Holy Father John Paul II has indicated that, in order to highlight the Christological content of this Marian devotion, five new mysteries, the "mysteries of light", should be added to the fifteen traditional mysteries.

Holy Rosary, written in 1931, naturally contains no reference to these new mysteries. But throughout his life St Josemaría lovingly contemplated and preached on these scenes, just as he did with every chapter of the Gospels. Therefore we have included here some excerpts from the writings of the Founder of Opus Dei that make reference to the luminous mysteries, to help readers meditate on the complete Rosary.

We can show our fidelity to the spirit of the author of *Holy Rosary* when we pray the joyful, luminous, sorrowful and glorious mysteries by uniting ourselves to the intentions of the successor of Peter, the Bishop of Rome. *Omnes cum Petro ad Iesum per Mariam!*

† Javier Echevarría
Prelate of Opus Dei
Rome, 14 February 2003

THE FIRST MYSTERY OF LIGHT

THE BAPTISM OF OUR LORD

*T*hen Jesus came from Galilee to the Jordan to John, to be baptized by him...and lo, a voice from heaven, saying, "This is my beloved Son, with whom I am well pleased" (Matt 3:13,17).

In Baptism, God our Father has taken possession of our lives. He has made us sharers in Christ's life and sent us the Holy Spirit.

The strength and the power of God light up the face of the earth.

We will set the world ablaze, with the flames of the fire that you came to enkindle on earth! And the light of your truth, our Jesus, will enlighten men's minds in an endless day.

I can hear you crying out, my King, in your strong and ardent voice: *ignem veni mittere in terram, et quid volo nisi ut accendatur?* I have come to bring fire to the earth, and would that it were already enkindled! —And I answer, with my entire being, with all my senses and faculties: *ecce ego: quia vocasti me!* Here I am, because you have called me!

God has placed an indelible mark on your soul through Baptism: you are a child of God.

Child, are you not aflame with the desire to bring all men to love Him?

Sources: *Christ is passing by,* 128; *Intimate notes,* 1741; *The Forge,* 264, 300.

THE SECOND MYSTERY OF LIGHT

THE WEDDING FEAST AT CANA

Our Lady was a guest at one of those noisy country weddings attended by people from many different villages. Mary was the only one who noticed the wine was running out. Don't these scenes from Christ's life seem familiar to us? The greatness of God lives at the level of ordinary things. It is natural for a woman, a homemaker, to notice an oversight, to look after the little things that make life pleasant. And that is how Mary acted.

Do whatever he tells you.

Implete hydrias (John 2:7), fill the jars. And the miracle takes place. Everything is so simple and ordinary. The servants carry out their job. The water is easy to find. And this is the first manifestation of our Lord's divinity. What is commonplace becomes something extraordinary, something supernatural, when we have the good will to heed what God is asking of us.

Lord, I want to abandon all my concerns into your generous hands. Our Mother – your Mother – will by now have said to you, as at Cana: "They have no wine!..."

If our faith is weak, we should turn to Mary. Because of the miracle at the marriage feast at Cana, which Christ performed at his Mother's request, *his disciples learned to believe in him* (John 2:11). Our Mother is always interceding with her Son so that he may attend to our needs and show himself to us, so that we can cry out, "You are the Son of God."

—Grant me, dear Jesus, the faith I truly desire. My Mother, sweet Lady, Mary most holy, make me really believe!

Sources: *Christ is passing by*, 141; *Letter,* 14 September 1951, 23; *The Forge*, 807; *Friends of God*, 285; *The Forge*, 235.

THE THIRD MYSTERY OF LIGHT

THE PROCLAMATION OF THE
KINGDOM OF GOD

The kingdom of God is at hand; repent, and believe in the gospel (Mark 1:15).

And all the crowd gathered about him, and he taught them (Mark 2:13).

Jesus sees the boats on the shore and gets into one of them. How naturally Jesus steps into the boat of each and everyone of us!

When you seek to draw close to our Lord, remember that he is always very close to you, that he is in you: *regnum meum intra vos est* (Luke 17:21). The Kingdom of God is within you. You will find him in your heart.

Christ should reign first and foremost in our soul. But in order for him to reign in me, I need his abundant grace. Only in that way can my every heartbeat and breath, my least intense look, my most ordinary word, my most basic feeling be transformed into a hosanna to Christ my King.

Duc in altum. —Put out into deep water! —Throw aside the pessimism that makes a coward of you. *Et laxate retia vestra in capturam.* And pay out your nets for a catch!

We have to place our trust in our Lord's words: get into the boat, take the oars, hoist the sails and launch out into this sea of the world which Christ gives us as an inheritance.

Et regni ejus non erit finis. –His kingdom will have no end.

–Doesn't it fill you with joy to work for such a kingdom?

Sources: *Notes from preaching*, 19 March 1960; 1 January 1973;
Christ is passing by, 181; *The Way*, 792;
Christ is passing by, 159; *The Way*, 906.

THE FOURTH MYSTERY OF LIGHT

THE TRANSFIGURATION

*A*nd he was transfigured before them, and his face shone like the sun, and his garments became white as light (Matt 17:2).

Jesus, we want to see you, to speak to you! We want to contemplate you, immersed in the immensity of your beauty, in a contemplation that will never cease! It must be wonderful to see you, Jesus! It must be wonderful to see you and be wounded by your love!

And a voice from the cloud said, "This is my beloved Son, with whom I am well pleased; listen to him" (Matt 17:5).

Lord, we are ready to heed whatever you want to tell us. Speak to us: we are attentive to your voice. May your words enkindle our will so that we launch out fervently to obey you.

Vultum tuum, Domine, requiram (Ps 26:8). Lord, I long to see your face. I like to close my eyes and think that, when God wills, the moment will come when I will be able to see him, not as *in a mirror dimly, but...face to face* (1 Cor 13:12). Yes, *my heart yearns for God, the living God. When shall I go and behold the face of God?* (Ps 41:3).

Sources: *Notes from preaching,* 4 June 1937; 25 July 1937;
25 December 1973.

THE FIFTH MYSTERY OF LIGHT

THE INSTITUTION OF THE EUCHARIST

*N*ow before the feast of the Passover, when Jesus knew that his hour had come to depart out of this world to the Father, having loved his own who were in the world, he loved them to the end (John 13:1).

When our Lord instituted the Eucharist during the Last Supper, night had already fallen. The world had fallen into darkness, for the old rites, the old signs of God's infinite mercy to mankind, were going to be brought to fulfilment. The way was opening to a new dawn – the new Passover. The Eucharist was instituted during that night, preparing in advance for the morning of the Resurrection.

Jesus has remained in the Eucharist for love ... for you.

–He has remained, knowing how men would treat him ... and how you would treat him.

–He has remained so that you could eat him, and visit him and tell him your concerns; and so that, by your prayer beside the tabernacle and by receiving him sacramentally, you could fall more in love each day, and help other souls, many souls, to follow the same path.

Good child: see how lovers on earth kiss the flowers, the letters, the mementos of those they love...

Then you, how could you ever forget that you have him always at your side – yes, *Him*? How could you forget ... that you can eat him?

–Lord, may I never again flutter along close to the ground. Illumined by the rays of the divine Sun – Christ – in the Eucharist, may my flight never be interrupted until I find repose in your Heart.

Sources: *Christ is passing by*, 155. *The Forge*, 887, 305, 39.

The Five Joyful Mysteries
(Mondays and Saturdays)

1st: The Annunciation.

2nd: The Visitation.

3rd: The Birth of our Lord.
4th: The Presentation.
5th: The Finding in the Temple.

The Five Mysteries of Light
(Thursdays)

1st: The Baptism of our Lord.
2nd: The Wedding feast at Cana.
3rd: The proclamation of the Kingdom of God.
4th: The Transfiguration.
5th: The Institution of the Eucharist.

The Five Sorrowful Mysteries
(Tuesdays and Fridays)

1st: The Agony in the Garden.
2nd: The Scourging at the Pillar.
3rd: The Crowning with Thorns.
4th: The Carrying of the Cross.
5th: The Crucifixion.

The Five Glorious Mysteries
(Wednesdays and Sundays)

1st: The Resurrection of our Lord.
2nd: The Ascension of our Lord.
3rd: The Descent of the Holy Spirit.
4th: The Assumption.

5th: The Crowning of the Blessed Virgin.